LITTLE BOOKS
ABOUT
BIG
THINGS

FREEMASONS

WASHINGTON AS A FREEMASON.

LITTLE BOOKS
ABOUT
BIG
THINGS

FREEMASONS

Bob Bailey Mucker

FALL RIVER PRESS

New York

FALL RIVER PRESS

New York

An Imprint of Sterling Publishing
387 Park Avenue South
New York, NY 10016

Cover design by Igor Satanovsky
Book design by Gavin Motnyk

ISBN 978-1-4351-4684-6

Distributed in Canada by Sterling Publishing
c/o Canadian Manda Group, 165 Dufferin Street
Toronto, Ontario, Canada M6K 3H6
Distributed in the United Kingdom by GMC Distribution Services
Castle Place, 166 High Street, Lewes, East Sussex, England BN7 1XU
Distributed in Australia by Capricorn Link (Australia) Pty. Ltd.
P.O. Box 704, Windsor, NSW 2756, Australia

For information about custom editions, special sales, and premium and
corporate purchases, please contact Sterling Special Sales at 800-805-5489
or specialsales@sterlingpublishing.com.

Manufactured in Canada

2 4 6 8 10 9 7 5 3 1

www.sterlingpublishing.com

Picture Credits:
Shutterstock: 9, 10, 92, 147, 158, 164, 188
Wikimedia: 146, 156, 157, 180, 185

INTRODUCTION

reemasonry is fascinating because it's mysterious. It's this perceived mystery that often causes problems when outsiders start to believe that a "secret society" chooses to remain "secret" because it's up to no good. Recent books and movies, such as *The Lost Symbol* and *National Treasure*, have sensationalized the Masons and fed those suspicions—often unfairly and without basis. That's why, in recent years, Masonic Lodges around the world have regularly opened their doors to non-members during special events and "open house" days. So, if you've ever wanted to set foot inside a Masonic Lodge, you just might have your chance. (Check your local Lodge website for details.)

The Masons (also known as Freemasons) still have unusual rites and rituals that have endured for centuries. Many of these practices seem strange to non-Masons, but most have reasonable explanations. As for the history of the "Craft," it is complicated and fascinating, and there certainly are aspects of Freemasonry that few people will ever understand. Scholars devote their entire careers to studying Masonic history and lore; facts and issues are forever debated. Some answers have been lost forever; others are hiding and waiting to be discovered. Still others can be found in the pages of this little book.

Freemasons trace their roots to the stonemasons of ancient and medieval times—the men who, literally, built the world, from King Solomon's Temple to the cathedrals of Europe. It is generally accepted that modern Freemasonry originated with the guilds of professional stonemasons in Europe. Guilds had requirements for membership and rules of conduct by which members had to abide, just as Masonic Lodges do today.

Some Masonic historians believe that Germany can lay claim to the world's oldest Masonic societies. Records show that Masonic organizations, whose members all were working stonemasons—also known as Operative Masons—existed in Germany in the 12th century.

The first "Grand Lodge" might have been formed as early as 1250 during the construction of the Cologne Cathedral. The first convocation of Masonic Lodges probably took place in Strasburg in 1275.

The oldest Masonic document in existence is the Regius Manuscript, an epic poem reputedly written in Middle English that is said to date from 1390. According to tradition, the Regius Manuscript describes the origins and rules of Freemasonry (although why these would have been documented in a 794-line poem is anyone's guess).

James Orchard Halliwell-Phillipps, a mathematician and Shakespeare scholar, found and translated the manuscript in 1839–40.

Thus the Regius Manuscript is also known as the Halliwell Manuscript. Today, it is one of the many Masonic documents in the collection of the British Library in London.

𝕿he last four words of the Regius Manuscript are "So Mote It Be." They also happen to be the four most recognized words in Freemasonry. Masonic Lodge meetings traditionally open and close with the phrase, "So Mote It Be," a sort of Masonic "amen." The word "mote" is thought to be an Anglo-Saxon version of the word "may."

"*So Mote It Be*"

A Masonic Lodge with deep roots is Lodge of Edinburgh No. 1 in Scotland. It has in its Lodge archives recorded minutes of a meeting conducted in 1599 and a document known as the Schaw Statutes that contains Masonic regulations from 1598. This Lodge is still active today and its history goes back to the stonemasons' guilds of the Middle Ages.

Magic Number

1717

1770 was the year that Modern—or "Speculative"—Freemasonry began. Not every man who is a Freemason today is an "Operative" Mason (a working stonemason). June 24, 1717, marked the official chartering of what is known today as the United Grand Lodge of England (U.G.L.E. for short), the first Masonic organization to have members who were known as Speculative Masons because they were not stonemasons by profession.

Υou'll often see the words "Free and Accepted Masons" (or the abbreviation F. & A.M.) following the name of a Masonic Lodge. This is another legacy of the modern age of Freemasonry. Interpretations of the phrase vary, but essentially:

Free and Accepted *Masons*

"Free" means that a Brother has joined of his own free will and that he was not enslaved or forced into Freemasonry; "Accepted" means that even though a Brother is not a stonemason by trade, he has been accepted into the Craft.

The first Masonic Lodge in the United States was chartered in Boston in 1733.

Henry Price, an English Freemason who'd settled in the colonies, found a number of fellow Masons in Boston with nowhere to meet. So he returned to the Grand Lodge of England and requested permission to establish a Masonic Lodge in North America. The English Brothers not only gave him their blessing, they made Henry Price the first Provincial Grand Master in North America.

That Lodge eventually became the Grand Lodge of Massachusetts.

he Lodge that Henry Price established in 1733 met in an upstairs room at the Green Dragon Tavern in Boston. The St. Andrews Lodge also met there. Among the members were two names you'll recognize: Paul Revere and John Hancock. And it seems that in 1773 those Masonic Brothers gathered together to do more than socialize and observe Masonic rites. . .

*T*here's plenty of reason to believe that the Masonic Brothers of the St. Andrews Lodge met at the Green Dragon Tavern to plan the Boston Tea Party.

We can speculate but we don't know for certain who participated in the raid on December 16, 1773. Still, the names that come up on the lists of likely candidates include quite a number of men known to be Freemasons.

If the Grand Lodge of England had known what was coming, would it ever have chartered a colonial Lodge?

$\mathcal{W}$hat many people—even many Masons—are surprised to learn is that right around the same time and in the same city another important Masonic milestone was occurring. That is the start of Prince Hall Masonry, the branch of Free and Accepted Masons founded by and largely populated by men of color.

Its story begins in 1775 with a man named Prince Hall. . .

Q So Prince Hall was a real person?

A Indeed he was. Prince Hall was a free black man living in Boston before the Revolutionary War. In 1775, he and 14 other free black men were admitted into Irish Lodge No. 441, a Lodge affiliated with the British infantry posted to the colonies.

Their acceptance marked the first time that men of color were made Masons in the United States.

*W*hen the British forces were leaving the colonies in 1776 (after a little matter of war), Prince Hall and his American Brethren were given permission to form their own Masonic Lodge with certain rights and privileges, and Prince Hall was named its Master.

In 1784 that Lodge petitioned the Grand Lodge of England (even after the war all things Masonic stemmed from England) for the full rights of all Free and Accepted Masons. The request was granted and African Lodge No. 459 of Boston was officially chartered.

The Boston Lodge was so successful, Prince Hall was named Provincial Grand Master and he went on to found African Lodge No. 459 in Philadelphia and Hiram Lodge No. 3 in Providence, Rhode Island.

After his death in 1807, African Grand Lodge No. 1 in Boston was renamed Prince Hall Grand Lodge in his honor. Today there are some 5,000 Masonic Lodges and 47 Grand Lodges that trace their lineage directly to the Prince Hall Grand Lodge of Massachusetts.

esides rising to prominence in the Masonic community, Prince Hall was an important figure in the fight against slavery and in the establishment of schools for black children. He also famously petitioned General George Washington to extend free black men the right to join the colonial army.

Modern Freemasonry from its very beginning has been populated by men of good character who are civic-minded, charitable, and dedicated to the service of others.

To become a Mason one must:

BE A MAN;

BE OF LEGAL AGE;

BELIEVE IN A SUPREME BEING;

APPROACH THE LODGE
OF HIS OWN FREE WILL;
AND
BE RECOMMENDED BY TWO MEMBERS
OF THE LODGE IN GOOD STANDING

Masons don't recruit new members. In fact, Brethren traditionally are forbidden to approach anyone—even family members and friends—with an offer to become a Mason. According to the Masonic Service Association of North America, "Freemasonry is bigger than any man; the man must seek its blessings; it never seeks the man." So men who would like to become Masons must ask a Brother "of [his] own free will and accord" for an opportunity to become a Mason.

Q If Masons aren't allowed to talk about Freemasonry to the public, how does one identify a Mason?

A The first thing to look for is a ring, lapel pin, watch fob, necklace, or other accessory bearing the Masonic square and compass. Only Brethren who have reached the degree of Master Mason are permitted to wear such items bearing Masonic symbols, so if you spot one you can expect the wearer is a member of the Craft. In fact, one reason Master Masons wear Masonic rings is so members of the public can identify them as Masons.

Many Master Masons also wear Masonic rings to make themselves known to other members of the Craft and to remind themselves of their commitment to Freemasonry.

The way the ring is worn can indicate the Brother's intention. If the ring is worn with the compass tips pointed toward the tips of the fingers, the wearer wants others to recognize him as a Mason. If the ring is worn with the compass tips pointed toward the wrist, he wishes to remind himself that he is a Master Mason.

Some Masons choose more unusual means of identifying themselves. A man who works as a tattoo artist had several clients request Masonic tattoos. He became curious enough to ask them about Freemasonry and eventually he became a member of the North Hollywood (California) Lodge No. 542. The identifying insignia might have been unorthodox, but they did what they were intended to do!

The states of Illinois and Missouri are among those that offer specialty license plates bearing the Masonic Square and Compass that denote a Master Mason. To order the license plates, you must show proof that you have ascended to the degree of a Master Mason.

Magic Number

1,336,503

There were 1,336,503 Freemasons in
the United States in 2011. Masonic
membership hit its peak in the
United States in 1959 when 4,103,161
American men belonged to Masonic
Lodges. It has been declining ever
since.

—Membership figures from the Masonic Service
Association of North America

*W*orldwide Freemasonry membership has been in decline for decades. So Masonic Lodges are working to raise their profiles among the general public, open their doors, and lift the "veil of secrecy" around them. They don't actively recruit, but they are working to make themselves more accessible to non-Masons who want to learn about Freemasonry.

The idea is to bring in new Masons and to make it clear to the world that Freemasonry has nothing to hide—except some members-only passwords and bits of arcana, but we'll get to that. . .

Three Primary Degrees of Freemasonry

1° Entered Apprentice

2° Fellowcraft

3° Master Mason

First Degree (1°) Mason is known as an Entered Apprentice. The term goes back to the Middle Ages, when young men would apprentice with a master craftsman—such as a stonemason—to learn a particular trade. After a period of time the apprentice would be asked to demonstrate his knowledge of the craft. If he passed the test, he would be promoted. An Entered Apprentice in a Masonic Lodge today must answer a series of questions to demonstrate his knowledge of Freemasonry and gain a promotion to Second Degree.

You've probably heard the expression "being hoodwinked." Did you know it relates to Freemasonry? During the initiation ceremony for an Entered Apprentice, the candidate is blindfolded—or "Hoodwinked"—before being led into the ceremonial chamber. In Freemasonry, Hoodwinking is not meant to deceive the candidate. It represents the candidate's move from the "profane darkness" to the "light" of the Craft.

hoodwinking also makes a candidate completely dependent on the Masons who are about to welcome him into the Brotherhood. That's symbolic, too. The candidate trusts his Brethren to keep him safe and to lead him where he needs to go. It has been said: "The purpose of the Hoodwink is not to hide things from the candidate. There is nothing to hide. Moreover, all that there is is later on revealed, for the Hoodwink is removed in the early part of the ceremonies. The Hoodwink is to be used to bring about a certain state of mind. . ."

Before an Entered Apprentice candidate enters the Lodge room his clothing is altered so that he is "neither naked nor clothed, neither barefoot nor shod." Typically a candidate takes off one shoe, rolls up a trouser leg so his leg is bare, and slips one arm out of his shirt so half his chest is bare. This places him in "distress" and reminds him that if he ever sees a Brother in distress he's obliged to help.

"I led them with cords of kindness, with bands of love."

In addition to being Hoodwinked, an Entered Apprentice candidate is fitted with a rope called a cable tow that is tied around his neck and used to lead him into the Lodge room. This practice comes from the Biblical Book of Hosea, 11:4, which says "I led them with cords of kindness, with bands of love." The cable tow symbolizes the connection Freemasons have with each other.

Magic Number
24 Inches

The 24-inch gauge is the first symbolic
tool given to an Entered Apprentice.
It resembles a ruler that is divided into
three sections of eight inches each.
Working stonemasons would have used
such a gauge to measure their work, but
Freemasons see the 24-inch gauge as a
symbol of how to measure the 24 hours
in a day—eight hours in devotion to God
and the service of others, eight hours for
work, eight hours for rest.

The Entered Apprentice is also given a Common Gavel and a Chisel, the ancient stonemason's most basic tools. A stonemason uses a gavel and chisel to chip away the rough edges of a piece of stone until it fits a space smoothly and snugly. For a Freemason the Common Gavel and Chisel symbolize the need to chip away bad habits and the rough edges of one's personality.

Second Degree (2°) Masons are called Fellowcrafts. Freemasonry is the Craft and they are fellows—not quite Master Masons (that comes later) but more experienced than Entered Apprentices. If he were an Operative Mason a Fellowcraft might be called Journeyman.

$\mathcal{J}$ust as an Entered Apprentice is given simple tools to symbolize his connection to the Craft, a Fellowcraft is given tools that represent his advancement in the Craft. They are the Square, the Level, and the Plumb, and they symbolize the importance of proper behavior and conduct both within the Lodge and outside it.

A working mason would use a Level to ensure that a wall is perfectly horizontal and flat. For a Freemason, the Level symbolizes that all men are equals—on the same level—and should be treated with the same consideration in one's business and personal life.

A working mason would use a Plumb to judge when a wall is vertically true—straight up-and-down. For a Fellowcraft, the Plumb symbolizes uprightness. It reminds him to be honest and moral in his behavior toward others and not to bend or fall to the will of others.

The Square is used by working masons to gauge whether the walls of a building are positioned properly so that the corners are perfectly square. If the walls are out of position, the building is weakened and could topple. For a Fellowcraft, the Square serves as a reminder that he must strive for order and harmony in his behavior and his dealings with others.

The Third Degree (3°) of Freemasonry is the Master Mason. For many Masons, this is the highest degree they will attain. Masonic lore compares the three fundamental degrees of Freemasonry to the three stages of a man's life: youth, adulthood, and old age.

he lessons of the Master Mason degree relate to the passage of time and how important it is not to waste a moment of precious life. Once a Brother has learned the lessons of the Entered Apprentice and the Fellowcraft, as a Master Mason he puts them into practice, making sure he treats others fairly—or, as the Masons would say, squarely—helps those in distress, and lives an upright life.

Magic Number

Ecclesiastes

12

Chapter 12 of the Old Testament Book of Ecclesiastes is read at the ceremony in which Brethren are raised from Fellowcraft to Master Mason. The passage, which is known as "The Whole Duty of Man," concerns the judgment of man at the end of his life. It says: "Fear God, and keep his commandments: for this is the whole duty of man."

The Trowel is one of the tools of the Master Mason. It symbolizes the Master Mason's ability to spread the "cement" of brotherly love. This refers to the Masonic brotherhood, but also to the world as a whole. Master Masons identify themselves to the world as Masons, by the tokens they wear and by the way they behave. In a sense they are ambassadors for Freemasonry.

The time it takes for a Mason to progress from Entered Apprentice to Fellowcraft to Master Mason varies. It can be as little as a few weeks. In some cases though, the Brother chooses to take his time in each degree, learning about Freemasonry, his Lodge, and his fellow Brethren. Meetings and activities may be exclusive for each degree, allowing Brethren to bond with others who are new to the Craft.

Magic Number
33°

The highest degree of Freemasonry is 33°. An Entered Apprentice is considered a First Degree (1°) Mason; Fellowcraft is Second Degree (2°); and Master Mason is Third Degree (3°). But Freemasonry doesn't stop there.

Depending on the structure and affiliation of his Lodge, a typical Mason may rise as high as 32° Mason, Master of the Royal Secret.

The 33° Mason, Sovereign Grand Inspector General, is an honorary degree conferred on an individual for his service to Freemasonry.

In simplest terms, the Scottish Rite is Freemasonry's version of "continuing education." Master Masons (3° Masons) may join the Scottish Rite to further their Masonic enlightenment and rise to 4° Mason and so on up to 32° Mason.

There are specific requirements for joining the Scottish Rite and they won't have much significance to you unless you're already a Freemason. One thing that is worth noting, however. . .

Masonic historians can't determine the connection between the Scottish Rite and Scotland.

They have traced the roots of the Scottish Rite back to 1730, when it was referred to as an advanced degree of Freemasonry. It was mentioned in records from England and France, but whatever link it might have had with Scotland is now shrouded in mist like the Scottish highlands.

he York Rite and Royal Arch also continue a Master Mason's Masonic education and confer "advanced" degrees different from those in the Scottish Rite.

The distinctions between these governing bodies are complicated, unless you've progressed far enough in Freemasonry for them to be relevant. And if that's the case, you'll already have acquired the necessary knowledge to understand them.

Such knowledge is what separates true Masons from cowans. . .

Q What is a cowan?

A A cowan is a phony Mason, a poser, an eavesdropper, or a Mason of a lower degree, such as an Entered Apprentice, who tries to pretend he knows more than he does. The name probably comes from an old Scottish word, although that's not clear. What is clear, however, is that no one likes a cowan.

Q   What is a Tyler?

A   A Tyler is an official doorkeeper of a Masonic lodge. His primary job is to keep out cowans—interlopers, eavesdroppers, fakes, phonies, and anyone who doesn't belong in the Lodge, especially during official activities and ceremonies.

To gain admittance, a Mason must demonstrate to the Tyler that he belongs to a Lodge, sometimes with a special knock on the door or by reciting an oath that only a genuine Mason would know.

It's unlikely that a Masonic Lodge today would be infiltrated by cowans, but it sometimes happens. . .

Masonic imposters—men who pretend to be members of the Craft but are not—have been a problem throughout the history of modern Freemasonry. For a man to be admitted into Freemasonry, he had to be of demonstrated good character. If he was a bad egg, he would not be accepted. And if he went ahead and tried to pretend he was a Brother when he was not, that would pretty much make clear just what a bad egg he was!

The Prudence Book of Freemasonry for 1859, written by Dr. Rob Morris, one of the great Masonic writers of all time, was intended as a guide to help individual Lodges detect imposters in their midst. His goal was ambitious: Morris wanted *The Prudence Book* to list the names of every single Freemason in the United States. (There were hundreds of thousands at the time.) If a man approached a Lodge claiming to be a Freemason, and he wasn't listed in *The Prudence Book*, the Lodge would have reason to be suspicious.

Q Why would someone pretend to be a Freemason?

A The short answer is: money. As in most fraternal organizations, Freemasons are taught to behave charitably toward Brethren in need. (This lesson begins from the very moment a candidate for Entered Apprentice enters the Lodge.) Before insurance or work benefits were common, members of fraternal organizations relied on their Lodges for help in a crisis. Naturally, con men and fraudsters couldn't resist trying to grab some undeserved aid for themselves.

Magic Number

Low Twelve

In Masonic parlance, Low Twelve means midnight—the time when the sun is "below" the earth. Symbolically, Low Twelve indicates bad luck or sadness. The programs that many Masonic Lodges administer to pay benefits to a Brother's family after his death are typically known as Low Twelve Clubs.

A 1902 report from the Grand Lodge of Iowa told of a man named Robert James who "called upon the Brethren at Davenport and requested aid upon the strength of his alleged Masonic affiliations." The Lodge in Davenport contacted the Lodge in Idaho that James claimed was his fraternal home. That Lodge immediately "denounced him as an imposter and asked that he be arrested and held." Instead, James bolted to Rock Island, Illinois, where he tried his scam again. There he was arrested and jailed for obtaining money under false pretenses.

The Grand Lodge of Iowa concluded, "Masonic charity should be as broad as the mercy of God, but it should discriminate between a hypocritical, lying renegade and 'a worthy brother in distress.' These despicable tramps who have nothing of Masonry but the memory which clings to their disreputable selves . . . are deserving of the severest punishment which the law can inflict for fraud."

Masonic imposters became such a scourge in the 19th and early 20th centuries that descriptions and even photos of them would be published in newspapers (what the Masons called the "secular press") so that they could be recognized and apprehended by any member of the public—Mason or not.

he idea of a "secret handshake" or "grip" seems quaint or comical to some, but it has long been a way for Freemasons to identify themselves to each other. If you haven't been accepted into the Craft, you won't know the grip. (In theory, at any rate.) So, traditionally, shaking hands has been one way for Freemasons to detect an imposter.

Of course, the tricky part is detecting a former Mason—someone who was once a member of the Craft but who was expelled from Freemasonry due to his bad character or malfeasance. He might be well versed in grips and codes and other Masonic identification and still be a bad egg.

And speaking of bad eggs. . .

If there were a Masonic Hall of Shame, Benedict Arnold would be a charter member. The notorious Revolutionary War traitor might have become a Freemason in the West Indies, where he was engaged in business before the war. He then affiliated with Hiram Lodge No. 1 in New Haven, Connecticut, and was an active member until he betrayed the colonials. After that, he was stricken from the Masonic rolls—and the Lodge records with his name scratched out in pen prove it.

The most famous Masonic "crime" involved the disappearance of William Morgan in 1826. When he was denied membership in (or perhaps kicked out of) a Lodge in upstate New York, Morgan planned to write a book denouncing Freemasonry as a secret society that threatened the security of democracy. Since there were many men in positions of political influence at the time—including DeWitt Clinton, the governor of New York—the idea of a "tell-all" book exposing their alleged wrongdoing captured the imagination of the public. But Morgan had a checkered past. . .

everal Masons in his hometown of Batavia, New York, claimed that Morgan neglected to pay back money he'd been lent. It's not clear whether this was true, but Morgan was arrested and jailed for his debts. The next day, someone paid Morgan's bail and he was released. He left the jail in a carriage with two men and went to Fort Niagara on the banks of the Niagara River.

After that, William Morgan was never seen alive again.

*W*hen a body floated up from the Niagara River, people—including Morgan's wife—claimed it was his. But it wasn't. Nevertheless, it was agreed that Morgan had been kidnapped from jail that night by the men in the coach. Five Masons were arrested and sentenced for Morgan's kidnapping. His remains were never recovered. A monument erected in his memory stands in the Old Batavia Cemetery.

 ut the case of William Morgan didn't
end there. His disappearance led to a
passionate wave of Anti-Masonic sentiment
and the founding of the Anti-Masonic
political party, whose goal was to remove all
Masons from political office. In 1828, the
Anti-Masonic Party ran a candidate for
governor of New York.

In 1832 the Anti-Masonic Party held the first presidential nominating convention in American history and nominated former U.S. Attorney General William Wirt to run for the office of President of the United States. Now here's the ironic part. . .

William Wirt, the Anti-Masonic Party candidate for President of the United States, had been a Freemason. And although he had left his Lodge, he was not an outspoken critic of the Craft.

In the 1932 election, the Anti-Masonic Party had some influence, especially in Vermont where all Freemasons were voted out or excluded from office. Yet, despite that credible showing by the Anti-Masons, President Andrew Jackson was re-elected.

Jackson, the seventh President of the United States, was a Freemason and the former Grand Master of the Grand Lodge of Tennessee.

O ne of the most prominent Anti-Masons in American history was John Quincy Adams, the sixth President of the United States, whose 1847 book, *Letters on the Masonic Institution*, strongly lays out his case against Freemasonry. In essence, he claimed that Freemasonry divided a man's loyalty between Masonic laws and the laws of the United States. He used the case of William Morgan as evidence.

$\mathfrak{A}$nother prominent Anti-Mason in American politics was Millard Fillmore, who was elected to the New York State Assembly and the U.S. Congress as an Anti-Masonic Party candidate.

He ran as a candidate of the Whig Party when he was elected the 13th President of the United States.

William H. Seward was elected to the New York State Senate as an Anti-Masonic Party candidate in 1830. Thirty-seven years later, as secretary of state under President Andrew Johnson, Seward became legendary for his negotiation to purchase Alaska from Russia.

While many honorable and well-intentioned men considered themselves "Anti-Masons," there have been plenty more who opposed the Craft for selfish or evil reasons. The dictators Benito Mussolini of Italy, Francisco Franco of Spain, and Adolf Hitler of Germany all opposed Freemasonry and persecuted, jailed, or even executed members of the Craft.

Some (of Many) Bans Against Freemasonry

1737: King Louis XV bans Freemasonry in France.

1738: Pope Clement XII issues a Papal Bull prohibiting Catholics from becoming Freemasons.

1775: Bernardo Tanucci bans Freemasonry in the kingdoms of Naples and Sicily.

1801: Alexander I of Russia confirms a 1797 ban on all secret societies. He rescinds the ban in 1803 (and joins the Masons!). Then he reissues the ban in 1822.

1826: Nicholas I of Russia confirms the 1822 ban of Freemasonry.

1923: Benito Mussolini demands Masons resign from Freemasonry in Italy.

1939: General Francisco Franco bans Freemasonry from Spain.

Most official bans against Freemasonry have been rescinded over time (occasionally to be reinstituted), but the Catholic Church's position on Freemasonry remains unchanged since the Papal Bull issued by Pope Clement XII in 1738. He said allegiance to Freemasonry (or any other so-called "secret society") conflicts with obedience to the Catholic Church. He instructed Catholics to "stay completely clear of such Societies. . .under pain of excommunication."

Magic Number
1983

The Catholic Church's position on Freemasonry was reconfirmed in 1983. "The faithful who enroll in Masonic associations are in a state of grave sin and may not receive Holy Communion."

This declaration was issued by the Cardinal Prefect, Joseph Ratzinger. The cardinal went on to become Pope Benedict XVI in 2005.

eneral Francisco Franco, the Nationalist dictator, equated Freemasonry with Communism when he banned it from Spain in 1939. He used affiliation—or alleged affiliation—with Freemasonry as an excuse to imprison his political adversaries. But the association between Freemasonry and Communism was something Franco concocted in his mind.

In fact. . .

*W*hen the Bolsheviks took power during the Russian Revolution in 1917, they came down hard on Freemasonry. (Czar Alexander I banned Freemasonry in 1822, but it resurfaced in Russia briefly at the beginning of the 20th century.)

In 1922, at the Fourth Congress Communist International, led by Leon Trotsky, Freemasonry was banned from Russia—again. This time because it was said to represent elite values and bourgeois thinking.

In 1992, Freemasonry returned to Russia once again.

$\mathcal{B}$ecause Freemasonry involves all sorts of rituals and symbols, those outside the Craft have long been suspicious of it. The fact is most Masonic symbols have sensible explanations: even the mysterious All-Seeing Eye. The Freemasons didn't invent it. They didn't even place it on U.S. currency. The All-Seeing Eye is a religious and spiritual symbol that dates back to antiquity.

The All-Seeing Eye represents the eye of God, which watches over us, protects us, and makes sure we're behaving as we should. "The eyes of the Lord are on the righteous," is a line from Psalm 34, written in the time of King David.

The Eye of Horus is a protective symbol from ancient Egyptian mythology. Horus was the sky god. According to some interpretations of the myth, his right eye was the sun and his left eye was the moon. Besides offering protection, the Eye of Horus could bring prosperity and could restore health.

The watchful eye was also a symbol of the ancient Egyptian god Osiris, the benevolent god of the dead, and was part of the hieroglyphic of his name.

The amulet known as a hamsa, which is shaped like a hand with an eye in its palm, is a traditional protective symbol in Arabic and Jewish culture. It is sometimes called the Hand of Fatima, the Hand of Miriam, or the Hand of Mary. Regardless, it always contains an All-Seeing Eye that watches over and protects the wearer from harm.

 reemasons are quick to point out that the first recorded Masonic use of the All-Seeing Eye and the Pyramid symbols only date back to 1783, while the All-Seeing Eye in a triangle appeared in Christian paintings and on buildings hundreds of years earlier. It was recognized universally as a symbol of protection. So. . .

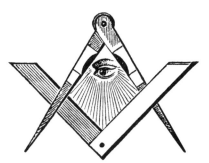

The All-Seeing Eye that appears on the reverse of the U.S. one-dollar bill symbolizes the hope that the nation would be watched over, guided, and protected by God. It is not—as any Freemason would strongly remind you—evidence of a Masonic plot to control the United States.

10 Masonic Symbols

1. *Square*

2. *Compass*

3. *Mosaic Floor*

4. *Pillars*

5. *Skull and Bones*

6. *Pilgrim's Sword*

7. *Trowel*

8. *Acacia*

9. *Coffin*

10. *Beehive*

𝕿he square and compass are the symbols that are best known and most closely identified with Freemasonry.

The square is a right angle. To a Freemason, it represents morality, truthfulness, and honesty.

The compass is an architect's or mathematician's compass (not the type used by a navigator). It represents restraint, skill, and knowledge.

 Q What letter appears inside the Masonic square and compass?

 A The answer is G, but the real question is "Why?" And the answer is that no one can say for certain.

Plenty of Freemasons would tell you that the G stands for God, which is a simple explanation, but perhaps too simple for something connected with Freemasonry (where very few things have simple explanations). So naturally there is another explanation. . .

The letter G inside the Masonic square and compass is most commonly thought to stand for Geometry. That is, the branch of mathematics most closely associated with architecture, order, and uprightness. An Operative Mason could not perform his work without the knowledge and use of geometry. The ability to make things square and true is just as important for a Speculative Freemason.

In some countries—France for example—the G more often appears inside a blazing star.

he Mosaic Floor is one of the earliest symbols of modern Freemasonry, although even the venerable Albert G. Mackey, among the most noted Masonic scholars of all time, can't say why: "The Masonic tradition is that the floor of the Temple of Solomon was decorated with a mosaic pavement of black and white stones. There is no historical evidence to substantiate this statement. . . By a little torsion of historical accuracy, the Freemasons have asserted [this]. . . hence, as the Lodge is a representation of the Temple, that the floor of the Lodge should also be of the same pattern."

Magic Number

The two pillars in Freemasonry represent the two pillars of King Solomon's Temple from biblical times. You'll see them depicted on Masonic regalia of all sorts, especially Masonic aprons. You'll also find two pillars standing tall within the ceremonial meeting room of a Masonic Lodge.

The pillars, including their dimensions—18 cubits tall and 12 cubits around—are specifically mentioned in the Bible (I Kings 7:15).

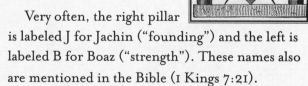

Very often, the right pillar is labeled J for Jachin ("founding") and the left is labeled B for Boaz ("strength"). These names also are mentioned in the Bible (I Kings 7:21).

References and symbols related to King Solomon's Temple are everywhere in a Masonic Lodge building, especially inside the ceremonial meeting rooms. Built in ancient Jerusalem to house the Ark of the Covenant, Solomon's Temple was the edifice by which all others were measured—the most splendid building in the world. And who built it? Masons, of course. Thus modern Speculative Masons have laid claim to it. And to one Master Mason in particular. . .

Q Who is Hiram Abiff?

A

1 Kings Chapter 7 in the Old Testament refers to a man called Hiram of Tyre, a widow's son from the Hebrew tribe of Naphtali. He was "filled with wisdom, and understanding, and cunning to work all works in brass. And he came to King Solomon and wrought all his work." 1 Kings goes on to outline Hiram's contributions to the building of the Temple in great detail. And from this, a Masonic legend was born.

Freemasons call Hiram of Tyre "Hiram Abiff" (Abiff is from the Hebrew word for "father"), and consider him the chief architect of King Solomon's Temple. His Masonic tale, briefly encapsulated, is this:

At the end of a workday Hiram Abiff was accosted by three ruffians who demanded that he reveal the secrets of a Master Mason to them. Such "trade secrets" had great value and Hiram refused to divulge them. When the thugs realized he wouldn't speak, they murdered Hiram Abiff.

Within Freemasonry, his story is a cautionary tale for all Master Masons.

To Freemasons, as to civilizations dating back to ancient times, the Skull and Bones symbolize man's mortality. They're not intended to be sinister; they simply serve as a reminder for Brethren to follow a proper code of behavior and to live righteously because their time on earth is limited. (The idea of using one's time wisely is a recurring theme in Freemasonry.)

Nevertheless, like the All-Seeing Eye, the Skull and Bones symbol used by Freemasons has been a source of wild speculation for decades.

Q

Those university Skull and Bones secret societies are Masonic brotherhoods, right?

A

For the record, neither the Yale University Skull and Bones "secret society" (founded in 1832) nor the Penn State University Skull and Bones Honor Society (founded in 1912 and entirely independent of the Yale society) are affiliated with the Freemasons.

There will forever be those who insist otherwise. Even the fact that the Penn State Skull and Bones has admitted women since 1974, and Yale Skull and Bones since 1992, won't change the skeptics' minds.

To Freemasons, as to most people, the coffin is a symbol of mortality.

It's usually depicted with a sprig of acacia beside it—acacia being a symbol of the everlasting life and purity of the soul. In Egyptian mythology acacia was the tree of life. In the Bible, acacia wood was used to build the Ark of the Covenant. For Freemasons, acacia symbolizes innocence and the idea that if one lives a righteous life his soul can achieve immortality.

The beehive is a symbol of industriousness. Who's busier than a bee? So the hive reminds them to devote themselves to work—diligently and cooperatively. Freemasons didn't invent the concept of the hive as a symbol for work. There's evidence of that from ancient Egypt. But some Masonic scholars have pointed out that the beehive is a particularly appropriate image for Freemasons because *building* is the specific thing that keeps bees busy—just as building keeps Operative Masons busy.

Q Why do Freemasons wear aprons?

A

The Masonic apron represents
the leatherwork aprons worn
by stonemasons in ancient and
medieval times. When a Brother
becomes an Entered Apprentice he
is given a white apron, usually made
of lambskin, to symbolize purity
and innocence. As he proceeds
to the degrees of Fellowcraft and
Master Mason his apron will
be decorated with symbols that
indicate his degree within the
Craft, offices he holds or has held,
and other things of significance.

Although today's Masonic aprons may be made of all sorts of materials—and Brethren who forget their aprons have been known to enter meetings with a handkerchief tucked in their waistbands as substitute aprons!—the traditional material for a Masonic apron is lambskin.

Early Masonic aprons were ankle length and had a bib to cover the wearer's chest, like a true working apron. As time went on, the style evolved. For a while they were worn with the bib unfastened and flapping down in the front. Later the apron was shortened and a flap added at the top.

he wives and sisters of Masonic Brothers often were the ones who decorated their Masonic aprons with embroidery or paint. Some enterprising women saw a business opportunity in the making of Masonic regalia. The Scottish Rite Masonic Museum and Library has more than 40 aprons and items made in the early 20th century by Miss Rose Lipp of Boston, Massachusetts, a specialist in the custom tailoring and decoration of "society regalia."

I ndividual Lodges sometimes add their own signature touches to their Masonic aprons. Lodge Han Yang No. 1048 in Seoul, South Korea, chartered in 1908 by the Grand Lodge of Scotland, trims its aprons with the MacFarlane Ancient Hunting Tartan as a tribute to a founding member and Right Worshipful Master of the Lodge.

Some Famous Masons' Aprons and Where to Find Them

Winston Churchill
Library and Museum of Freemasonry, London

Henry Howard Molyneux Herbert,
4th Earl of Carnarvon
British Library, London

Meriwether Lewis
Grand Lodge of Montana Museum and Library

Voltaire
Freemasonry Museum in Paris

George Washington
Grand Lodge Museum in Philadelphia

George Washington
Mt. Nebo Lodge No. 91 in West Virginia

The great circus entrepreneurs, the Ringling Brothers—all seven of them!—were members of Baraboo Lodge No. 34 in Baraboo, Wisconsin. On one special occasion, they were presented with matching aprons trimmed with pale blue silk, embroidered and decorated with silver thread, and stamped with each Ringling Brother's name. (Some say the aprons were sewn by the costumers from the circus.)

The Ringling Brother's aprons dropped out of sight for a time. Then, to everyone's surprise, they came up for sale on the Internet. Today the Ringling Brothers' aprons are in the collection of Baraboo Lodge No. 34.

An 18th-century Royal Arch apron owned by the Scottish poet Robert Burns was put up for auction at Bonhams London in 2009. The apron was made of white chamois leather backed by blue silk and covered with hand-painted decoration. Estimated price was $23,000 to $39,000, but it was not sold. It remains in a private collection.

An embroidered silk apron that belonged to George Washington is on display in the Grand Lodge Museum at the Masonic Temple in Philadelphia.

Tradition says that the apron was embroidered by the wife of the Marquis de Lafayette as a gift for Washington. It depicts more than 40 Masonic symbols, including the Square, the Compass, and the All-Seeing Eye.

A second Masonic apron that was given to Washington by Lafayette is the prized possession of Mt. Nebo Lodge No. 91 in Shepherdstown, West Virginia. It was given to the Lodge in 1815 by Captain Thomas Hammond, who was married to Washington's niece Mildred.

The Washington apron from Mt. Nebo Lodge No. 91 was worn by the architect Robert Mills in 1848 at the laying of the cornerstone for the Washington Monument in Washington, D.C.

Geeorge Washington was initiated as an Entered Apprentice in Fredericksburg Lodge No. 4 of Fredericksburg, Virginia, in 1752. During the Revolutionary War, more than 90 Masonic Brothers from Fredericksburg Lodge No. 4 fought on the colonial side— seven of them as generals.

When he was elected president of the United States in 1789, Washington was also serving as Master of Alexandria Lodge No. 22 (now known as Alexandria-Washington Lodge No. 22) in Alexandria, Virginia.

Q

Why do people think Freemasons control the world?

A

Who knows? It's true that the rolls of Freemasons over the centuries have included many prominent men: kings, princes, presidents, and prime ministers. Not only political leaders, but business leaders, too. Henry Ford was a Mason; so were Walter Chrysler and John Jacob Astor. But if Freemasons really did control the world, Masonic politicians wouldn't be defeated—or overthrown—by non-Masons (that's not the case) and more men would be clamoring to become members of the Craft (that's not the case either).

Some Freemasons do get up to no good, and when they happen to be in positions of authority their crimes and misdeeds become widespread news. Those stories make Freemasons cringe because they know that no matter what the circumstances some people will be determined to pin the blame on Freemasonry.

Freemasons are used to the backlash, but that doesn't mean they like it. They know every organization has its good guys and its bad guys. They prefer to focus on the good.

Masonic World Leaders

Salvador Allende
Former president of Chile

Edmund Barton
First prime minister of Australia

Simón Bolívar
Venezuelan independence leader, former president of Colombia

Winston Churchill
Former British prime minister

King George VI of England

Benito Juárez
Former president of Mexico

Francisco de Miranda
Venezuelan revolutionary

Bernardo O'Higgins
Chilean independence leader

José de San Martín
Argentinean independence leader

Freemasonry fosters connections, and that was especially true at Logia Lautaro, sometimes called the Lodge of the Rational Knights. Formed in Cadiz, Spain, (probably) and named for a 16th-century Mapuche leader who fought to kick the Spanish conquerors out of Chile, Lautaro Lodge met secretly and plotted to do precisely the same thing. It's also likely that there was more than one Lautaro Lodge, creating a network between Spain and Latin America.

Its members included many of the men who liberated Latin America from Spain: Simón Bolívar, Bernardo O'Higgins, José de San Martín, and Francisco de Miranda, who founded the Lodge.

U.S. Presidential Masons

George Washington

James Monroe

Andrew Jackson

James K. Polk

James Buchanan

Andrew Johnson

James Garfield

William McKinley

Theodore Roosevelt

William Howard Taft

Warren G. Harding

Franklin Roosevelt

Harry Truman

Gerald Ford

Robert R. Livingston, a jurist, politician, and Grand Master of the Grand Lodge of Free and Accepted Masons of the State of New York, administered the presidential oath of office to George Washington on April 30, 1789, in New York City. When taking the oath, Washington placed his hand on the Bible of the St. John's Lodge No. 1.

The George Washington Inaugural Bible was later used at the inaugurations of Warren G. Harding, Dwight D. Eisenhower, Jimmy Carter, and George H.W. Bush. When it's not in use for ceremonial occasions, it is on display at Federal Hall in New York City.

Magic Number

10,000

This is the number of Freemasons listed
in the book *10,000 Famous Freemasons*
written by William R. Denslow, with a
foreword by Harry S. Truman. Both
Denslow and Truman were Fellows and
Past Masters of the Missouri Lodge
of Research, a group dedicated to
the research, study, and preservation
of Masonic history. The book was
published in four volumes between 1957
and 1960. It was reissued in 2007.

*W*arren G. Harding, the 29th president of the United States, was admitted to Freemasonry at Marion Lodge No. 70 in Marion, Ohio, in 1901, but his path into Freemasonry wasn't easy. Harding was blackballed—rejected—several times before his application was accepted. Blackballing is rare in Freemasonry, and Harding suffered its effects (it is said) because of unfounded rumors about his heritage and because his Republican party politics didn't mesh with the Democratic views of his region.

Magic Number

19 years
1 month
16 days

This is the length of time between Warren G. Harding's induction as an Entered Apprentice and his progression to Fellowcraft. Typically, an Entered Apprentice passes to Fellowcraft within weeks. For Harding, the delay was caused by Brethren who opposed him politically. He abandoned his pursuit of Freemasonry until he began his presidential campaign. On August 13, 1920, he was passed to Fellowcraft and on August 27 he was raised to a Master Mason.

On November 2, 1920, Harding was elected President of the United States.

Q

Is it true that a woman has never become a Freemason?

A

Not necessarily. The best-documented case of a female Freemason is that of an Irish aristocrat named Elizabeth St. Ledger (or St. Leger; later Mrs. Richard Aldworth). As a teenager, she walked in on a Lodge meeting being conducted by her father in their home. Apparently Elizabeth saw and heard too much for an outsider, so the Brethren decided to make her a Freemason, which would obligate her to secrecy.

There's a portrait of Elizabeth Aldworth née St. Ledger wearing Masonic regalia, and the Provincial Grand Lodge of Munster, in Cork, Ireland, has her Masonic apron in its collection. Within Freemasonry, she's known as "Brother Elizabeth."

nother case of a female Freemason involves Helene, Countess Hadik Barkoczy, of Hungary. In the mid-19th century when her father died, Helene was his only heir. The Hungarian court ruled that she was entitled to a full inheritance—precisely the same as what a son would have received—and included in her inheritance was a library of Masonic literature. Helene started reading and she became fascinated by Freemasonry. She asked for admission to a local Masonic Lodge and she was admitted in 1875.

However. . .

The Grand Orient of Hungary, which oversaw the Lodge that admitted Helene, was furious about the decision, which it said violated the basic laws of Freemasonry. The Grand Orient immediately issued a demand for her to return whatever documents or gifts she had received from the Lodge and it expelled the Lodge leadership from Freemasonry forever.

ow here's an ironic twist for you. . .

The Lodge that admitted Countess Helene was called Lodge Egyenloseg. It still operates in Budapest, Hungary, today.

The word Egyenloseg means "Equality" in English.

From time to time there are stories of Masonic Lodges that have started to allow women to become Entered Apprentices. (Recent news from France comes to mind.) Although the reports might make it seem as if such a decision was sanctioned by all Freemasons everywhere; that's not the case. Dig a little deeper and you'll find that these erstwhile Masonic Lodges are acting independently and are not recognized by the Grand Lodge of their country or, perhaps, any other.

*W*hich brings us to Masonic pedigree. . .

The Symbolic Lodge (or Blue Lodge) is the unit of Freemasonry on a local level. A recognized (also known as approved) Masonic Lodge admits a candidate as an Entered Apprentice and allows him to proceed to Fellowcraft and rise to Master Mason. The Brother in charge of the Lodge has the title of Worshipful Master (W.M. for short) and his second- and third-in-command are called Wardens. They're all elected by the members of the Lodge.

S ymbolic Lodges must be chartered by a Grand Lodge with jurisdiction over their geographic location. In the United States, most states have a Grand Lodge but there is no "Grand Lodge of the United States."

Other countries have their own Grand Lodges (or Grand Orients), sometimes more than one, that determine the rules and practices for the Symbolic Lodges. They may differ slightly, but their adherence to fundamental Masonic rules is consistent. So, a lodge that decided to disregard a basic Masonic rule by, say, allowing women to become Freemasons, would lose its charter pronto.

enerally speaking, every Grand Lodge on earth can trace its lineage to the United Grand Lodge of England. The English and the Scottish (who have their own very ancient Grand Lodge) were responsible for carrying Freemasonry throughout the world. As it took hold, Symbolic Lodges applied for charters from the Grand Lodge of England. When there were enough of them in a particular place, a Grand Lodge was formed and that too was chartered by G.L.E. (Grand Lodge of England).

Here's an example. . .

The Grand Lodge of Iowa traces its lineage like this:

The Grand Lodge of North Carolina received its Charter from the Grand Lodge of England in 1787.

The Grand Lodge of Tennessee received its Charter from the Grand Lodge of North Carolina in 1813.

The Grand Lodge of Missouri received its Charter from the Grand Lodge of Tennessee in 1821.

The Grand Lodge of Iowa received its Charter from the Grand Lodge of Missouri in 1844.

Q **Why do Masonic Lodges have numbers?**

A The number indicates the order in which Symbolic Lodges were chartered by a particular Grand Lodge. Typically, the older the Lodge, the lower the number. To make sure this was the case in South Africa, when the Grand Lodge of South Africa was chartered in 1952 it went back and re-chartered the oldest lodge in the country, Lodge of Good Hope, which had operated since the 1700s.

Today the Lodge of Good Hope is No. 1 on the register of the Grand Lodge of South Africa.

Masonic Auxiliary Organizations

The Order of the Eastern Star
for women with Masonic affiliations

....

International Order of the Rainbow
for young women

....

International Order of Job's Daughters
for young women

....

Order of DeMolay
for young men

....

Dr. Rob Morris, whose name comes up quite often in Masonic history, believed that women as well as men should benefit from the principles and fellowship of Freemasonry. Of course the rules of Freemasonry are very clear about who may or may not be a member of the Craft. So Morris created a type of Masonic ladies' auxiliary that he called the Order of the Eastern Star. That was in 1850.

Magic Number

500,000+

This is the number of members under the Grand Chapter of the Order of the Eastern Star. Both men and women may be members of the Eastern Star. All of them have ties to Freemasonry. Most of the men are Master Masons. The women are wives, sisters, mothers, and others who are related to members of the Craft.

International Order of the Rainbow for Girls was created in 1922 for the daughters of Masons and Shriners. Today any young woman between the ages of 11 and 20 may join.

Job's Daughters was founded in 1920 and takes its name from the Book of Job, 42:15: "In all the land were no women found so fair as the Daughters of Job, and their father gave them inheritance among their brethren." Membership is open to young women, ages 10 to 20, who are direct descendants of a Master Mason.

O rder of DeMolay, for young men aged 12 to 21, is named for Jacques de Molay, the last leader of the Knights Templar. Frank Land founded the organization in Kansas City in 1919 as a sort of junior Freemasons organization that would teach younger men the virtues and codes by which Freemasons live their lives.

Famous DeMolays
(but not Masons)

Reubin Askew
Former governor of Florida and U.S. trade representative

Mel Blanc
The voice of Bugs Bunny and many other cartoon characters

Frank Borman
Apollo 8 astronaut and former CEO of Eastern Airlines

Bill Clinton
42nd president of the United States

Walt Disney
Arts and entertainment visionary

Mark Hatfield
Former U.S. senator and governor of Oregon

Harmon Killebrew
Major League Baseball Hall-of-Famer

Pete Rose
Major League Baseball star

John Steinbeck
Pulitzer Prize–winning author, The Grapes of Wrath

Fran Tarkenton
NFL Hall of Fame quarterback

Magic Number
10

The 10 rubies on the DeMolay emblem represent Frank Land, the organization's founder, and the nine young men who were its first members back in 1919. Originally, the stones were pearls, but Land intended that they be changed to rubies as each of the ten entered into "the adventure beyond this life."

The first DeMolays were: Louis G. Lower, Ivan M. Bentley, Edmund Marshall, Gorman A. McBride, Jerome Jacobson, William W. Steinhilber, Elmer Dorsey, Clyde C. Stream, and Ralph Sewell.

*J*acques de Molay, for whom the organization is named, joined the Knights Templar in 1265 when he was just 21 years old. He rose through the ranks to become a Grand Master during the Crusades, but became the chief victim of another type of crusade waged by French King Philip IV. Philip the Fair, as he was called, wanted to wipe out the Knights Templar (and to appropriate their considerable treasury). He imprisoned Jacques de Molay and his cohorts, tried them, and sentenced them to be burned at the stake.

Q So there's a direct connection between Freemasons and the Knights Templar?

A No. Maybe. Yes. In the 12th century, some European Christian knights relocated to Jerusalem to defend what had been claimed in the Crusades. They called themselves the Poor Knights (or Soldiers of Christ) of the Temple. "Poor" because they took a vow of poverty. "The Temple" was the Temple of Solomon. They grew and thrived—the poverty vow was eventually disregarded—but with the execution of Jacques de Molay, the Knights Templar dissolved, dispersed, or went into hiding.

No Freemasonry connection so far. . .

no one knows what happened next because when the Templars went AWOL they turned themselves into one of the great mysteries of human history.

One theory says that the remaining Templars went to Scotland at the invitation of Robert the Bruce, the Scottish king who was engaged in fighting the English and was grateful for the Templars' help. They did their work, stuck together and, for some unexplained reason, began referring to themselves as Freemasons.

It's a tale that won't go away, but most historians dismiss it as fiction.

More likely is the idea that some 18th-century Freemasons with vivid imaginations thought it was more romantic to associate their fraternity with knights on horseback spreading the word of God than with medieval guilds of stonemasons spreading mortar on bricks.

It's certainly true that some modern Masonic symbolism and ritual was adapted from medieval chivalry. But as for a direct connection. . .you'll have to keep looking.

One more thing. . .

The modern Order of Knights Templar is a worldwide association of Christian Freemasons of the York Rite.

It is especially known for the Knights Templar Eye Foundation, which raises funds for ophthalmology research and treatment. And it defines itself very clearly and officially as having "no proof of direct connection between the ancient order and the modern order known today as the Knights Templar."

Acacia is a college fraternity with Masonic roots. It was founded in 1904 at the University of Michigan in Ann Arbor by 14 students who also happened to be Master Masons. Acacia brothers today don't have to be Masons to join—they don't even have to pursue Freemasonry after they graduate, although many of them do. Acacia is a social organization, but it's also a service organization much like a Masonic Lodge.

Notable Acacia Brothers

Hiram Bingham III
Explorer of Machu Picchu (Yale, 1915)

William Jennings Bryan
U.S. Secretary of State (Nebraska, 1908)

Clifton Hillegass
Creator of CliffsNotes study guides (Nebraska, 1938)

Jack Kilby
Nobel Prize laureate, Physics (Illinois, 1942)

William Howard Taft
President of the United States (Yale, 1913)

Frank S. Land
*Founder of DeMolay, was made an honorary Acacia
at the University of Missouri in 1959*

*U*niversity men may, of course, enter Freemasonry once they are of legal age, and there are several Masonic Lodges with university ties. Two of the more notable are Isaac Newton University Lodge No. 859 in Cambridge, England, and Apollo University Lodge No. 357 at Oxford.

The Harvard Lodge, founded in 1922, was the first "academic lodge" in the United States. Its membership is limited to those with a connection to Harvard University.

The first academic lodge in the Commonwealth of Virginia opened in 2011—fittingly enough at George Mason University.

The Irish writer Oscar Wilde, whose works include *The Importance of Being Earnest* and *The Picture of Dorian Gray*, became a Freemason while he was a student at Oxford University in England. The certificate documenting his achievement was issued on December 20, 1876, by Apollo University Lodge No. 357—the Lodge for Oxford students. It is now in the Manuscript Collection of the British Library.

Eight Literary Masons

Robert Burns
Scottish poet, "Auld Lang Syne"

....

Arthur Conan Doyle
Creator of Sherlock Holmes

....

Johann Wolfgang von Goethe
German writer, dramatist, and poet, "The Mason's Lodge"

....

Rudyard Kipling
*First English-language writer to receive
the Nobel Prize for Literature*

....

Sir Walter Scott
Author of Ivanhoe

....

John Steinbeck
American author, The Grapes of Wrath

....

Mark Twain
American author, The Adventures of Tom Sawyer

....

Oscar Wilde
Irish playwright and satirist

....

"The Mason's Lodge," written by Johann Wolfgang von Goethe in 1827 is one of the best-known Masonic poems. Its first stanza has been translated several ways. Here are two:

> *"The Mason's ways are*
> *A type of existence,*
> *And his persistence,*
> *Is as the days are*
> *Of men in this world."*

> *"The mason's ways*
> *Are a symbol of life,*
> *And his toil*
> *Resembles the strife*
> *Of man on earth."*

Goethe was initiated at the Lodge Amalia in Weimar, Germany, in 1780. It's said that he requested not to be blindfolded—or Hoodwinked—during his initiation and asked that the Brethren accept his promise to keep his eyes shut during the ceremony instead.

Freemasons enthusiastically claim Robert Burns, the beloved Scottish poet, as one of their own. Among his best-known works is the poem called "Masonic Song":

"Within this dear mansion,
may wayward Contention

Or withered Envy ne'er enter;

May secrecy round be the mystical bound,

And brotherly Love be the centre!"

Burns was indeed a devoted member of the Craft. But his Masonic history was steeped in a rivalry that continues to this day. . .

Shortly before Robert Burns became an Entered Apprentice in July 1781, St. David Tarbolton No. 174 and St. James No. 178 Lodges decided to merge. Robert Burns was the only Masonic candidate to enter the joint Lodge known as St. David. He was raised to Master Mason in October 1781, but following some internal strife the two Lodges split apart again soon after. Burns went with the Brethren of St. James.

The Lodges' rivalry continues today: Lodge Tarbolton (Kilwinning) St. James No. 135 claims to be "The Lodge of Robert Burns." Lodge St. David Tarbolton (Mauchline) No. 133 calls itself "Burns's Mother Lodge."

Magic Number
100

George Markham Tweddell wrote 100 Masonic sonnets but unless you're a Freemason, you've probably never heard of him. That's a shame because the volume of poetry he published in 1887 is a heartfelt tribute to the Craft. As he writes in his first sonnet:

"I fain would sing—a humble Sonneteer—
The charms of Masonry: which, to my mind,
Comprises all that benefits mankind,
And can our troubled spirits truly cheer"

"Comprises all that benefits mankind. . ." Masons would agree with that sentiment.

Samuel Langhorne Clemens, better known as Mark Twain, became a Master Mason of the Polar Star Lodge No. 79 in St. Louis, Missouri, on July 10, 1861. He wasn't very active in the Lodge, but in 1868 he left it a legacy: a ceremonial gavel with this inscription:

"This mallet is of Cedar cut in the Forest of Lebanon whence Solomon obtained the Timbers for the Temple. The handle was cut by Brother Clemens himself from a cedar planted just outside the walls of Jerusalem . . . The gavel in its present form was made at Alexandria, Egypt, by order of Bro. Clemens."

Q Edgar Allan Poe: Freemason or Anti-Mason?

A Probably neither. Poe was mysterious and Freemasonry is mysterious, so naturally people assume a link between the two. Was Poe a Mason? There's no evidence to say so. Was he an Anti-Mason? That's not clear; but it's certain that Poe was aware of the philosophical conflict between the Catholic Church and the Freemasons. His 1846 story "The Cask of Amontillado" involves a Catholic and a Freemason, one of whom murders the other. (No spoilers, but in typical Poe style, no one gets off easy.)

James Joyce was not a Freemason, but Leopold Bloom the main character of his epic novel *Ulysses* was. Here's evidence from a conversation about Bloom:

"— Nosey Flynn made swift passes in the air with juggling fingers. He winked.

— He's in the craft, he said.

— Do you tell me so? Davy Byrne said.

— Very much so, Nosey Flynn said. Ancient free and accepted order. He's an excellent brother. Light, life and love, by God. They give him a leg up. I was told that by a—well, I won't say who.

— Is that a fact?

— O, it's a fine order, Nosey Flynn said. They stick to you when you're down. I know a fellow was trying to get into it. But they're as close as damn it. By God they did right to keep the women out of it."

Another great "was he or wasn't he?" subject is Leo Tolstoy. He wasn't, but the question arises because of his 1869 novel *War and Peace*. The book's description of Pierre Besukhov's initiation into the Freemasons was so sympathetic and so accurate! There's no evidence that Tolstoy himself was a Freemason—so how did he know so much about the secret ceremonies of the Craft?

𝕿he French writer, dramatist, and philosopher Voltaire, author of *Candide*, became an Entered Apprentice at the Lodge of the Nine Sisters (Loge des Neuf Soeurs) in Paris on April 4, 1778, less than two months before he died. It's said that his friend Benjamin Franklin, a noted Freemason, persuaded Voltaire to enter Freemasonry.

Ohe Philalethes Society is a group of Masonic authors dedicated to Masonic education and research. It was founded in 1928 at the Masonic Library in Cedar Rapids, Iowa, and takes its name from the Greek for "lover of truth." Patterned after the Academie Francaise, it is limited to forty Fellows at any one time.

Rudyard Kipling was a founding member of the Philalethes Society.

$\mathcal{Q}$ Was Sherlock Holmes a Freemason?

 $\mathcal{A}$ No, but his creator, Sir Arthur Conan Doyle, was a Freemason, and he used Masonic references in many Holmes stories. In "The Adventure of the Norwood Builder" he writes:

". . .You mentioned your name, as if I should recognize it, but I assure you that, beyond the obvious facts that you are a bachelor, a solicitor, a Freemason, and an asthmatic, I know nothing whatever about you."

Familiar as I was with my friend's methods, it was not difficult for me to follow his deductions, and to observe the untidiness of attire, the sheaf of legal papers, the watch-charm, and the breathing which had prompted them. Our client, however, stared in amazement.

Sir Arthur Conan Doyle was initiated into Freemasonry in 1887. Although Doyle eventually withdrew from Freemasonry, he famously—in Masonic lore, anyway—attended a Lodge meeting with Rudyard Kipling at Bloemfontein in South Africa during the Boer War.

Upon returning to the U.K., Doyle gave a speech at a Masonic event in which he recounted stories of soldiers on opposing sides of the conflict treating each other with more respect and care if they discovered that both were Freemasons.

Such tales are more common than you might expect. . .

10 Military Masons

Arthur, Duke of Wellington

Omar Bradley

Richard E. Byrd

Admiral David Farragut

John Paul Jones

Douglas MacArthur

General George McLellan

Robert Peary

Matthew Perry

John Joseph Pershing

The Marquis de Lafayette was a Mason, although when and where he was initiated is still disputed. Some say he was initiated at Valley Forge when he came to fight for the colonial cause during the American Revolution. It's more likely though, that he was a member of the Lodge St. Jean de la Candeur in Paris. His name is on Lodge documents from 1775, before he arrived in North America.

Q. Was Napoleon a Mason?

A. Inconclusive. Masonic historians continue to search for documentary evidence of the French emperor's membership in the Craft. Although legend has it that he was initiated in France. . . or in Malta. . . or in Egypt. . . no one has found records to prove this. Napoleon certainly was friendly toward the Masons, possibly because he recognized that such a well-organized and directed group of citizens could be helpful to his cause.

napoleon's older brother Joseph, the King of Naples and of Spain, definitely was a Mason. He was initiated in 1805 and eventually became Grand Master of the Grand Orient of France. The other Bonaparte brothers, Louis, Jerome, and Lucien, also were members of the Craft.

*W*hen Napoleon's forces entered Egypt, they brought with them French culture and Freemasonry. The Isis Lodge, the first Masonic lodge in Egypt, was founded in 1798 by General Jean Baptiste Kléber, an officer in Napoleon's army.

There's a plaque at the Alamo dedicated to the Masonic Brethren who fought there during the siege in 1836:

James Bowie

David Crockett

Almaron Dickenson

William Barret Travis

Both Sam Houston and Stephen Austin were Masons as well.

So was General Antonio Lopez de Santa Anna, who led the Mexican Army against the Alamo and defeated the Texans.

egend has it that when Santa Anna was captured at San Jacinto and brought before Sam Houston, Houston spared his life because they were fellow Masons. Learned historians give three reasons why that's not true.

1. By killing fellow Masons at the Alamo, including many who were unarmed and had already been taken prisoner, Santa Anna had breached all Masonic obligations.

2. Military protocol dictated that he be taken prisoner and not simply executed.

3. As a political figure and military leader, he was more valuable to the Texans alive.

According to Niles McKinley Lodge No. 794 in Ohio, William McKinley, the 25th president of the United States, was introduced to Freemasonry during the Civil War after the Battle of Opequon in 1864:

"I went with our surgeon of our Ohio regiment to the field where there were about 5,000 Confederate prisoners under guard. Almost as soon as we passed the guard, I noticed the doctor shook hands with a number of Confederate prisoners. He also took from his pockets a roll of bills and distributed all he had among them. Boy-like, I looked on in wonderment; I didn't know what it all meant. . ."

McKinley continued:

"On the way back from camp I asked him:

'Did you know these men or ever see then before?'

'No,' replied the doctor, 'I never saw them before.'

'But,' I persisted, 'You gave them a lot of money, all you had about you. Do you ever expect to get it back?'

'Well,' said the doctor, 'If they are able to pay me back, they will. But it makes no difference to me; they are Brother Masons in trouble and I am only doing my duty.'

I said to myself, 'If that is Freemasonry I will take some of it for myself.'"

Although he was a major in the Union Army, McKinley was initiated at Hiram Lodge No. 21 in Winchester, Virginia, a Confederate state, by John B.T. Reed, a Confederate chaplain and Worshipful Master of the Lodge on May 1, 1865. Thanks to the tutelage of the Brethren, who included both Union and Confederate sympathizers, McKinley became a Fellowcraft later that evening and was raised to a Master Mason on May 3.

A memorial bearing the inscription "Friend to Friend—A Brotherhood Undivided" stands at Gettysburg and commemorates the stories of Masonic brotherhood that transcended the philosophical and political differences that divided the United States in the Civil War. It depicts Union captain Henry Bingham giving aid to wounded Confederate general Lewis Addison Armistead.

Masonic Sites You Can Visit

Chancellor Robert R. Livingston Masonic Library
New York City, New York

Freemason Hall
London, England

George Washington Masonic Memorial
Alexandria, Virginia

Hollywood Masonic Temple
Los Angeles, California

The House of the Temple
Washington, D.C.

Masonic Library and Museum
Philadelphia, Pennsylvania

Parc Monceau
Paris, France

Prince Hall Monument
Cambridge, Massachusetts

Rosslyn Chapel
Roslin, Scotland

Scottish Rite Masonic Museum and Library
Lexington, Massachusetts

Parc Monceau, commissioned by Philippe, Duke of Chartres (later Duke of Orleans) in the mid- to late-18th century, has been noted for its Masonic symbolism. (A pyramid-shaped garden folly!) The Duke was a Freemason—Grand Master of the Grand Orient of France—and it's said that Masonic Lodge meetings were sometimes conducted within the gardens of Parc Monceau.

The House of the Temple in Washington, D.C., is the headquarters of the Scottish Rite of Freemasonry. The building was designed by John Russell Pope, who also designed the Jefferson Memorial and the National Archives, and it was inspired by the Mausoleum at Halicarnassus, one of the Seven Wonders of the Ancient World. Far from being clandestine, the House of the Temple has been open to the public ever since its completion in 1915.

Rosslyn Chapel became world famous—or perhaps infamous—thanks to *The Da Vinci Code*. While many of the novel's "facts" are up for debate, it certainly is true that the fabulous 15th-century carvings within Rosslyn Chapel depict many characters and motifs that have Masonic connotations. There's also a figure of an angel playing the bagpipes, which isn't Masonic, but is highly amusing.

The George Washington Masonic Memorial in Alexandria, Virginia, commemorates his deep ties to the Masons, and the Masons' reverence for the "Father of Our Country." Washington was the first U.S. president to be a Mason, but not the last. The memorial contains an archive and a collection of historic Masonic artifacts.

The historic Masonic Hall in Hollywood, California, former home of Hollywood Lodge No. 355, opened in 1921 at 6840 Hollywood Boulevard across from Grauman's (now Mann's) Chinese Theatre. It's said that the two buildings were connected by a secret tunnel that might have been used to hide liquor during Prohibition or by movie stars who wanted to sneak away unnoticed from premieres at the theater.

𝕿he two-story Hollywood Masonic Temple was designed by architect John C. Austin, whose firm also designed the Griffith Park Observatory and the Shrine Auditorium in Los Angeles. Today the building is owned by the Walt Disney Corporation and it is used as a theater, event space, and television studio.

Hollywood Lodge No. 355 now meets in Tarzana, California.

Twilight Zone creator Rod Serling and TV producer David Milch have stars on the Hollywood Walk of Fame outside the Hollywood Masonic Temple. So do recording artists Little Richard, Paul Anka, Mahalia Jackson, and Roy Clark. Cinematic special effects creator Ray Harryhausen has a star at 6840 Hollywood Boulevard. Movie star Donald Duck has one, too.

Roy Clark is the only notable name above who is a Freemason.

Hollywood Freemasons

Bud Abbott

Gene Autry

Ernest Borgnine

George M. Cohan

Cecil B. DeMille

W.C. Fields

Clark Gable

Michael Richards

Roy Rogers

Red Skelton

John Wayne

Magic Number
233

The 233 Club—also known as the Two Thirty-Three Club—was an organization of Freemason actors, directors, producers, and others in the Hollywood film industry. It had more than 1,000 members and in 1926 it announced plans to construct a $1.5 million, 13-story Lodge building in Hollywood. The building was to contain a theater, swimming pool, gymnasium, library, and bank, plus several floors of guest rooms and a roof garden with a dance floor and promenade.

Famed architect H. Roy Kelley was retained to design it, but it was not completed.

"ffinity" Lodges attract members who have a common bond besides Freemasonry. There are, for example, Lodges for men in a particular profession, for alumni of a particular secondary school or college, and for those who are in or have retired from military service.

Some Lodges are united by common language, others by common experience. There's even an international Lodge that conducts most of its daily business on the Internet.

Some Masonic Affinity Lodges

Authors' Lodge No. 3456
England: Founded in 1910 for literary types

Civil War Lodge of Research No. 1865
Virginia: For those researching the role of Masons in the U.S. Civil War

Fraternity Lodge No. 54
Washington, D.C.: For members of Greek letter college fraternities

Justice Lodge No. 457
Kansas: For those in law enforcement

Knights of Solomon Lodge No. 764
North Carolina: For Masons who ride motorcycles

Shotokan Karate Lodge No. 9752
England: For those with an interest in martial arts

Telephone Lodge No. 3301
England: For Masons in the telecommunications business

Daylight Lodges were mainly created to serve Brethren who work at night—such as printers and newspapermen back in the good old days. There also are daylight Lodges for elderly Masons who prefer not to travel to Lodge activities at night. And while it's unusual for ordinary Masonic Lodges to conduct meetings during the day, some do so purely out of tradition. Lodges formed more than a century ago were not necessarily equipped with electricity and daytime meetings were simply a practical choice.

St. Cecile Lodge No. 568 in New York City is known as the Lodge of the Arts, and its Brethren are musicians, actors, singers, and others in the performing arts. Chartered in 1865 and named for the patron saint of music, St. Cecile Lodge was conceived as a daylight Lodge because its members work at night.

Famous alumni of St. Cecile Lodge No. 568 include Harry Houdini, Paul Whiteman, Louis B. Mayer, William S. Paley, and Al Jolson.

F rancesco Geminiani, an 18th-
century Italian violinist and
composer, became a Freemason in
London in 1725. Shortly after that, he
formed *Philo-musicae et architecturae societas
Apollini*, a club for Freemasons who
played, or simply appreciated, music.
The society lasted just two years, but
the musical history of the Masons spans
centuries.

10 Musical Masons

Eddy Arnold

Count Basie

Irving Berlin

James Herbert "Eubie" Blake

George M. Cohan

Nat "King" Cole

Franz Joseph Haydn

Wolfgang Amadeus Mozart

John Philip Sousa

Mel Tillis

olfgang Amadeus Mozart was accepted into the Lodge Zur Wohltätigkeit (Beneficence) in 1784 in Vienna, Austria. By all accounts he was devoted to the Craft, giving it the greatest gift of all: his music. Among his compositions is a song used for the installation of new Freemasons, a composition called *Die Maurerfreude* (The Mason's Joy), and *Maurerische Trauermusik* (The Masonic Funeral Music). His 1791 opera *The Magic Flute*, for which fellow Mason Emanuel Schikaneder wrote the libretto, is filled with Masonic imagery and allegory.

$\mathcal{O}$he people of Austria, most of whom were Catholic, weren't comfortable with Freemasonry. According to some interpretations, *The Magic Flute* is said to convey the message that Freemasonry is harmless and fulfilling, and is appreciated best by those who are open-minded and tolerant.

Nevertheless, Freemasonry was banned in Austria from 1795 to 1867.

Some Masonic Lodges Named for Wolfgang Amadeus Mozart

Mozart Lodge No. 49 *(Lisbon; 1991)*
*Recently mentioned in connection with
a Portuguese government scandal*

....

Mozart Lodge No. 85 *(Tel Aviv; 2006)*
The first Russian–speaking Masonic Lodge in Israel

....

Mozart Lodge No. 121 *(New Jersey; 1871)*
*Founded by German–born and German–American Brethren in
Camden, New Jersey*

....

Mozart Lodge No. 436 *(Philadelphia; 1869)*
Founded as Philadelphia's first primarily musical Masonic Lodge

....

Mozart Lodge No. 1929 *(London; 1881)*
*The first Mozart Lodge in England, its motto is:
"Let Harmony Prevail"*

....

The book *10,000 Famous Freemasons* calls Jean Sibelius "the greatest Masonic composer since Mozart." He was one of the founding members of Suomi Lodge No. 1, the first Masonic Lodge chartered in Finland after the country gained its independence from Russia in 1918. His many compositions include the symphony *Finlandia*, and *Masonic Ritual Music*, a series of vocal and instrumental works he intended to be performed and heard only by Masons.

Q Was Beethoven a Mason?

A Unclear. Plenty of late-18th and early-19th century composers were Masons. Mozart, Haydn, and Liszt for starters. So it seems that Ludwig van Beethoven would be a likely member of the Craft. Unfortunately, no records exist that prove his membership in a Lodge—and Masonic Lodges are known for careful record-keeping. On the other hand, who knows what might have happened to such records during the past several hundred years. So the question of Beethoven's position in Freemasonry remains unanswered.

To appeal to the gentlemen in their concert audiences (many of whom were Freemasons) 18th-century composers were known to weave Masonic imagery into their work. The opera *Parsifal* by Richard Wagner and George Frideric Handel's *Orlando* both were influenced by Masonic lore, even though neither man was a member of the Craft.

Both William S. Gilbert and Arthur Sullivan, famed for operettas such as *The Pirates of Penzance*, *H.M.S. Pinafore*, and *The Mikado*, were Freemasons. They came to the Craft separately; however we have Freemasonry to thank for their musical partnership. They were introduced by Frederic Clay, a fellow composer and Freemason.

Arthur Sullivan Lodge No. 2156, consecrated in 1886 and now based near Manchester, England, was named for the composer.

country Singer Mel Tillis was raised to a 33° Mason at the House of Temple in Washington, D.C., in 1998. In addition to being an acclaimed singer and songwriter, and a member of the Country Music Hall of Fame and the Grand Ole Opry, he is a painter. Limited edition prints of his painting, "Masonic America," were sold to raise funds for the Scottish Rite Foundation, which benefits speech and hearing clinics in the United States.

Magic Number

The seven liberal arts and sciences are a recurring theme in Masonic ritual and lore. The fields of study were first defined in the Middle Ages and include grammar, rhetoric, logic, arithmetic, geometry, astronomy, and music.

While no one expects a Freemason to become a mathematician, an astronomer, or a musician (though many are), the emphasis on the seven liberal arts teaches Masons to have a respect for knowledge and encourages them to continue their education both within the Craft and in everyday life.

Freemasonry likes math. Students of the Craft find myriad ways to interpret the significance of numbers that recur in Masonic rituals and lore.

Seven is one number that comes up often. It is significant, some say, because it contains 3 and 4—the numbers of the perfect figures: the triangle and the square.

It took King Solomon seven years to build the Temple.

A spiral staircase of seven steps figures into Masonic ritual.

And Masons are taught that it takes "seven to make a Lodge perfect": a Master Mason, two Wardens, two Fellowcrafts and two Entered Apprentices.

Freemasons have been known to refer to God as "The Grand Geometrician of the Universe" or "The Great Architect of the Universe" (G.A.O.T.U. for short).

The Book of Proverbs 8:27 refers to God "setting a compass" upon the depths. If you're a Freemason, you'll find synergy in that.

Some Masons say that the letter G contained within the square and compass stands for the Grand Geometrician.

Classical Inspirations to Freemasonry

Archimedes
Ancient Greek scholar

Athena
Greek goddess of wisdom

Euclid
Ancient Greek mathematician, "Father of Geometry"

Minerva
Roman goddess of wisdom

Plato
Greek philosopher

Pythagoras
Ancient Greek mathematician

Vitruvius
Roman writer and architect

There are many Masonic Lodges named for mythological figures and ancient scholars. (Pythagoras is a particular favorite.)

Remember that old story about Archimedes who was in his bath when he hit on the principle of water displacement and jumped up shouting "Eureka!"? Well, that story probably is apocryphal, but regardless there are quite a few Masonic Lodges named Eureka. One of them is Eureka Lodge No. 20 in Seattle, which distinguishes itself as "Seattle's Masonic Lodge for Science Education," and is a major sponsor of the annual Washington State Science and Engineering Fair.

Medical and Scientific Masons

Edward Appleton
Physicist and Nobel laureate, first to identify the ionosphere

Luther Burbank
*Botanist who developed the Shasta daisy
and the Freestone peach*

Enrico Fermi
Nuclear physicist, Nobel laureate

Alexander Fleming
Biologist, Nobel laureate for the discovery of penicillin

Edward Jenner
Developed the cure for smallpox

Joseph Lister
Pioneer of antiseptic surgery

Hans Christian Oersted
Physicist, pioneer in electromagnetism

Joel Poinsett
Physician and botanist for whom the poinsettia flower is named

Luther Burbank Lodge No. 57 in Santa Rosa, California, Enrico Fermi Lodge No. 1046 in Pisa, Italy, and Joseph Lister Lodge No. 8032 in England (which folded in 2006) are among the Masonic Lodges named for Freemason scientists.

Isaac Newton University Lodge No. 859 in Cambridge, England, was named for the great mathematician and physicist. Lodge Copernicus No. 246 in Australia, Lodge Copernicus No. 505 in New Zealand, and Copernicus Lodge No. 545 in New York are named for the Polish astronomer.

Neither Newton nor Copernicus were Freemasons.

Q What's the connection between Masons and Shriners?

A All Shriners are Masons, but not all Masons are Shriners.

Back in 1872, two Master Masons in New York City conceived a Masonic-style Lodge that was purely dedicated to socializing and fun, without the solemn ritual of Masonic gatherings. Thus the Ancient Arabic Order of the Nobles of the Mystic Shrine—better known as the Shriners—was born. The fact that the group was not ancient, not Arabic, and not particularly noble didn't trouble them. They did institute one basic rule though: you must be a Mason to join the Shriners.

Shriners are known for their outlandish costumes and antics, from their characteristic red fez hats to their wacky performances in parades and festivals. What other group of grown men would take pride in driving around in tiny cars or go-karts?

They are also proudly devoted to philanthropic causes, especially those that help sick, crippled, or injured children.